*Praise for*

october 31

# 1517

## MARTIN LUTHER AND THE DAY THAT CHANGED THE WORLD

"Martin Marty provides valuable insights for the past, the present, and the future—why Luther's articulation of 'repentance' meant so much then, why his commitment to 'justification' has now built a bridge for Catholics and Lutherans to work with each other, and why this great event of 500 years ago might herald a hopeful future for Christian believers and all others. There is an awful lot packed readably into this one small book."

**—Mark Noll,** Francis A. McAnaney Professor of History, University of Notre Dame

"This volume is small but weighty."
**—Ray Olson,** in *Booklist*

"This book offers valuable insight on how Luther's 95 theses have had a profound influence on the ecumenical movement, and can help Christians today understand what it means to be a member of a truly catholic church."

**—Kathleen Norris,** award-winning poet and *New York Times* bestselling author of *Acedia & Me*

"Martin Marty, one of the world's preeminent scholars of religion, has written a succinct meditation on Martin Luther's Ninety-Five Theses, brilliantly summing up its history, its influence, and its meaning for us today, and it is a gem."

**—James Martin, sj,** Editor-at-Large, *America* magazine

"I would not dream of preparing my mind and heart for the celebration of Luther's role in the Reformation without finding out what Martin Marty has to say on the subject. And he says it here in this wonderful little book. Gifted historian that he is, Marty gives us much solid information. He also writes eloquently about how best to prepare our souls for the kind of commemoration that also includes some prayers of repentance."

**—Richard Mouw,** former President, Fuller Theological Seminary

MARTIN E. MARTY

october 31
1517

## MARTIN LUTHER
## AND THE DAY
## THAT CHANGED THE WORLD

FOREWORD BY JAMES MARTIN, SJ

PARACLETE PRESS
BREWSTER, MASSACHUSETTS

2017 First Printing Paperback Edition
2017 Fifth Printing Hardcover Edition
2016 First, Second, Third, and Fourth Printing Hardcover Edition

*October 31, 1517: Martin Luther and the Day that Changed the World*

Copyright © 2016 by Martin E. Marty

ISBN 978-1-64060-037-9

The Paraclete Press name and logo (dove on cross) are trademarks of Paraclete Press, Inc.

The Library of Congress has catalogued the hardcover edition of this book as follows:
Names: Marty, Martin E., 1928- author.
Title: October 31, 1517 : Martin Luther and the day that changed the world / Martin E. Marty.
Description: Brewster MA : Paraclete Press Inc., 2016. | Includes bibliographical references.
Identifiers: LCCN 2015051036 | ISBN 9781612616568
Subjects: LCSH: Luther, Martin, 1483-1546. | Luther, Martin, 1483-1546. Disputatio pro declaratione virtutis indulgentiarum. | Reformation—Germany—Sources.
Classification: LCC BR326.5 .M37 2016 | DDC 284.1092—dc23
LC record available at http://lccn.loc.gov/2015051036

10 9 8 7 6 5 4 3 2 1

Published by Paraclete Press
Brewster, Massachusetts
www.paracletepress.com

Printed in the United States of America

# CONTENTS

Y FAVORITE GENRE OF WRITING IS A short book on a big topic written by an expert. This is that kind of book. Martin Marty, one of the world's preeminent scholars of religion, has written a succinct meditation on Martin Luther's Ninety-Five Theses, brilliantly summing up its history, its influence, and its meaning for us today, and it is a gem. But what else would one expect from this peerless scholar and superb writer?

There is no little irony in a Jesuit writing a preface for this book (beyond the droll wordplay of James Martin on Martin Marty on Martin Luther). For the Jesuit Order, founded in 1540 and formally known as the Society of Jesus, is often, incorrectly, referred to as the "Shock Troops of the Counter-Reformation."

Like so much else written about the heated period known as the Reformation (or the Lutheran Reformation), this is inaccurate. St. Ignatius Loyola did not found the Jesuit Order in response to the Reformation.

In fact, as the Jesuit historian John O'Malley has pointed out in several books, for all the emphasis on the famous diptych of Luther on one side and Ignatius on the other, and for all the emphasis on the important role of the Jesuits in the Counter-Reformation (or the Catholic Reform), it is remarkable how infrequently the early Jesuits mention the Reformers in their letters and documents.

St. Ignatius's *Autobiography*, for example, written in large part to provide his fellow Jesuits with a detailed description of the spiritual background of the Society of Jesus, completely ignores the Reformation. Likewise, the Jesuit *Constitutions*, the overarching document meant to govern the Society and explain the nascent religious order to the church, to the world, and to the Jesuits themselves, mentions Luther and Lutheranism not at all.

What accounts for this? Mainly that Ignatius had a different purpose for setting up the Jesuits. It was not to counter the Reformers. Nor was it to serve as a bulwark against Lutheranism (though even many Jesuits may have thought so). Rather, Ignatius's original goal was simpler, and it was a goal that, ironically, closely unites him with Martin Luther. It was to "help souls."

The term "help souls" appears again and again in Ignatius's writings. And it is here that his life intersects rather poignantly with that of Martin Luther. For both men sought to help souls, though, as events transpired, in very different ways: one, though it was not his choice, by reforming the church from without; the other, though he would not have said it this way and certainly not publicly, by reforming the church from within.

Notably, both were appalled by the excesses of the Catholic Church at the time, though for different reasons. Now, it should be said that for Ignatius, who placed himself at the disposal of the pope and who once said that if the church said black was white he would have to agree, the Catholic Church was one of the centerpieces of his spirituality. Nonetheless, both he and Luther took dim views of church corruption. For Luther, the chief sin was the sale of indulgences, which were, in essence, "time off" from purgatory. Luther's horror of that malign practice is well known.

What is less known is what constituted an ecclesial horror for Ignatius. For him the chief sins of the church were clericalism, the attitude that views clerics as superior to all others, as well as careerism, which he saw as an absolute poison.

The founder of the Jesuits went so far as to require that all Jesuits making their Final Vows at the end of their long training period promise publicly that they would never strive for "high offices," either in the Society of Jesus or in the larger church. Moreover, if they had evidence of another Jesuit "ambitioning," they were to report him to the man's superiors. (That promise is still made by Jesuits today.) This was Ignatius's unique way of combatting church corruption.

Luther and Ignatius, then, were closer than one might think. Lutheran and Catholic reformers, if you will. And in recent years, happily, the two denominations, Lutheranism and Catholicism, have grown ever closer.

The signal grace of this indispensable book is that Professor Marty continues this reconciliation and shows us not only how Martin Luther's insights still speak to us but also how the differences between Catholics and Protestants serve to enrich our church. These differences, in fact, only underline the various ways both groups have sought to serve the one Lord, Jesus Christ, by, in their own ways, striving to "help souls."

# october 31
# 1517

MARTIN LUTHER
AND THE DAY
THAT CHANGED THE WORLD

# AN INVITATION

HIS IS AN INVITATION TO A PARTY, one that commemorates events that began five hundred years ago in Europe and have consequences throughout the world today. Throughout these pages, we shall frequently compare two things, a "heart" and a "soul." The story will deal with relations between the two, the first belonging to Martin Luther and those in his legacy, and the second to the Roman Catholic Church and those who belong to its community or communion.

Philosopher Eugen Rosenstock-Huessy observed that "any real book conveys one idea and one idea only." He had to know that many would disagree. After all, an encyclopedia or a catalog, for example, are full of many ideas. Nevertheless, an encyclopedia is ultimately indeed expressive of one idea, that of providing information, and the single idea of a catalog is to display.

"The good ones," the great classics or favored smaller books, are, finally, also about one thing. Think of *Pilgrim's Progress, Paradise Lost, Uncle Tom's Cabin, Little Women*, or for that matter *The Cat in the Hat*. While each may be full of many themes and things, each is finally about one integrating theme.

If readers are unable to find and tie together the strands of a narrative or the arguments of a book, their attention will wander, their memory will dim, and their ability to put the book to work for best advantage flags.

Whether or not this modest book is a "real" one is for others to judge, but it is indeed intended to be about just one thing. What that is should be made clear now, and then sustained along a thread of ideas that provide unity to the chapters that follow. The "one thing" that opens these pages relates to and, in fact, *is* the first of ninety-five theses that were proposed five hundred years ago by Martin Luther. That thesis prompted a collection of ideas, proposals, arguments, songs, and actions with which people wrestled or which they enjoyed both then and now, half a millennium after 1517. Here is that first thesis, as it was voiced by that influential monk in Germany half a millennium ago: "When our Lord and

Master Jesus Christ said, 'Repent' (Matthew 4:17), he intended the entire life of believers to be repentance."

So, simply put, this book is about "repentance" as a worthy theme for believers to keep in mind if and as they commemorate events of five hundred years ago, events that still shape many features of their lives.

# REPENTANCE HERE MEANS "A CHANGE OF HEART"

EPENTANCE" IS OFTEN A THEME OF commemorations, including those that occur annually in Jewish and Christian worship and lives. Those who participate in such worship know that, out of all their own sorrows and faults, and of those of others they recall, can come eventual healing and even joy. But getting to the positive points is difficult, thanks to bad public relations and personal resistance associated with "repentance."

In a world of anxiety, suffering, depression, and other "downs," we might well feel that there is no need for one more to serve as a centerpiece to an anniversary that comes around after five hundred long years. In today's world of advertising, entertainment, celebrity, and competition for favor, repentance loses out to "ups," which usually include promises of happiness, smiles, and success against whatever odds. Advertisers who regularly peddle pills that promote those "ups," celebrities who display giddiness, entertainers who they seek to distract, and high-achievers in general will not succeed if they get tied up in knots thinking about all they have done wrong, by anyone's standards—most notably, God's—as voiced by "Our Lord and Master, Jesus Christ," to use again the words of Matthew's Gospel, repeated by Dr. Luther.

Whoever agrees with this claim about the urgency of repentance cannot get off the hook by looking back to old ways. Jesus Christ willed "the entire life of believers" to be one of repentance. That life in its entirety typically has to include anniversaries of the posting of this first of Ninety-Five Theses. It does not mean that only on festival days or in sanctuaries or in the privacy of homes are believers to repent, but they are to do so in the whole of their existence. Whoever reads the Gospel stories of Jesus knows that the call to repent was his first word as he gathered followers to his Father's way. They know that he taught about the need for repentance among all sorts of people remembered in the Gospels.

Reflecting on the biblical career of his call can give us a sense of the problems "repentance" faces today. We think of what the word ordinarily images in our minds.

For those who heard Jesus, the seriousness of repentance reached the depths of their being. How did they respond? Their sacred Scriptures often enough called them to be realistic, to "go deep," to be freshly aware of what had gone wrong, to remember foreparents who "wore sack-cloth and ashes" and disfigured their faces so that they would remind themselves and others of their distance from God, from holiness. But such are by all means not the only scriptural images of the life of believers. Followers of Jesus are called to be and to show that they are free, God's children, people of promise who experience joy and spread it to others.

Repentance, then, rather than being only the practice of imprisoned criminals, people who isolate themselves in cells out in the desert, who compete with others to be virtuosos of gloom, crabby misfits in society, or celebrities caught in a scandal who have to admit a "mistake" in public, is a response to the promises of God, of grace. The biblical words for repenting, we recall, always involve a turning, an about-face, a basic change.

Think of repentance as a change of heart, which will be a constant when we are talking about what Luther was calling for in his first thesis. A modern thinker, the German philosopher Max Scheler, on whom the late

Pope Saint John Paul II wrote his own doctoral thesis, put much energy into this concept. Since the acts and thoughts that kept Luther (and keep us) bound and away from God belonged to the past (one cannot well repent of next year's sins!), it has to be asked, How can our repentance effect change, since we cannot change the past? That past is done, finished, closed.

What *can* be changed, and is changed in the act of repentance, and in an entire life of repentance, is one's attitude to the past as it affects the present. Believers today know that their ancestors often did terrible things. In a world of conflicts, many foreparents used power to build empires that led to the killing of millions of God's children in wars, the enslavement of others, the exploitation of the weak. But when believers are asked to repent, they cannot change the inherited past. They can only deal with the present, with today, which is why the confession of evil acts, thoughts, words, and ways is to occur daily.

In Scheler's spirit, the key question, implied in Luther's thesis about one's "entire life," whether an individual or a culture as a whole, is not, "Alas! What evil things did my ancestors do?" though that question may prompt fresh examination and not mere calls for revenge-against-ancestors voiced by people who are seeking someone to blame. Getting closer to home, is it a fully satisfying repentance if we only deal with the past, which cannot be changed? "Alas, what did I do?" I don't think so. Believers get closer to repentance instead by asking, "Alas, what kind of person was I that I could do that?" Still, what "I" was is now in the past, which again is over, closed.

So, the one who repents and seeks a change of heart asks, "Alas, what kind of person am I that I can do such bad things?" The divine response to repenting is the forgiveness of sins, which is what Luther thought the gospel is about. Believers of all stripes know that, but commemorations are excellent occasions to examine how repentance works in today's world.

People can repent en masse, when they ask what kind of persons they were that they could enslave or demean others. For an example from our own time: when Pope Francis meets crowds of millions he asks them to pray for a "change of heart," and to listen to the promptings of God so that they follow through with new resolves, new patterns. Likewise, when a pastor or priest hears the confession of a congregation or an individual and announces God's forgiveness, the act is meaningful to them only if the repentant parishioners or individuals have asked what kind of persons they are that they can do evil things—and if they accept the new way as a part of their "entire life" of repentance and forgiveness.

# CHAPTER three

## A FIVE-HUNDRED-YEARS-AGO ARGUMENT OVER "PENANCE"

HILE LUTHER GROUNDED THE FIRST of his ninety-five theses in the Gospels, it may seem difficult today to see why the Ninety-Five Theses should have had much, if any, influence in sixteenth-century Christian Europe. It was produced in the early career of a monk teaching in a new and probably still substandard little university in an obscure town in Saxony. We have to explore, to notice what nerve he touched, or, to change the metaphor, what fuse he lit. Find a university chapel door of your choice, tack up a piece of paper—or, in other accounts of 1517, open the mail in an archbishop's office—and read: that all believers should repent. Ho-hum. Yawn. Would the event be noticed?

In our time, cartoonists have regularly had fun inventing a character who seems to "fit the bill" of one doing Luther-like work today. He—it's always a "he"—is a long-haired, bearded, shabbily gowned, barefoot zealot or nut who is pictured bearing a sign with one huge word on it, *Repent!* Viewers of the cartoon are expected to smile at the irrelevant and eccentric figure. His real-life counterparts who stand on street corners and hand out pamphlets calling for repentance have a total of zero responders who listen and repent.

The reality is that through the centuries, serious believers in many places and times and contexts have had success with their call, and many did and still do repent. John the Baptist, Jesus's predecessor, started to make the call to which Jesus brought credentials, and that led to many successes. Later, believers of all ranks, including, notably, some well-known royal figures, often followed the call. In short, millions of simple believers have appraised their lives, responded to the call, and experienced grace and a "newness of life" that effected change.

Through their changed lives, they made history, and they still can and do. Spanish philosopher José Ortega y Gasset contended that "decisive historical changes do not come from great wars, terrible cataclysms, or ingenious inventions; it is enough that the heart of man incline its sensitive crown to one side or the other of the horizon."

In 1517, thousands of people in Saxony—and indeed in much of Europe—were ready to tilt the crowns of their hearts "to one side or the other." What came to be called the Protestant Reformation took hold, and various "counter-Reformations" followed. In other words, God had not, and has not, withdrawn the promises of a new life. Many thousands were repenting, undergoing a change of heart, and being forgiven. But there was discontent in the minds of many of those same people about how this change came about: through a system we often call the rites of penance. This is the nerve Luther touched.

In the modern world, people spend a great deal of energy reflecting on and living off of some so-called turning points in history. The American Revolution, which resulted in a "new birth of freedom," is an effective illustration. For decades, British colonists in North America were restless in the face of British policies that they experienced as enslaving, yet only July 4, 1776, is remembered as *the* day, as one day to represent hundreds of others, to commemorate the formation of a new nation. What happened in a hall in Philadelphia then had repercussions leading to the realizing of new liberties and establishing a national home where the people could flourish. The Emancipation Proclamation in the nineteenth century and legislation like the Voting Rights Act in the twentieth are further examples of turning points that produced more aftereffects.

So, some events of October 31, 1517, resulted from decades and more of discontent just as they anticipated, and in many ways led to, decades—indeed centuries—of eruptions, changing of hearts, wars, inventions of new policies and programs by those who would follow their Lord and Master Jesus Christ in repentance.

There are many ways to tell this story. Not a few library books or even libraries full of books include attacks on the very credibly attackable Luther and his colleagues. Some plausibly speak of an "accidental" or "incidental" or "unintended" Reformation. They blame it, not always without foundation, for wars—think of the Thirty Years' War (1618-48), which started as Protestants versus Catholics and eventually claimed, in many cities throughout central Europe, half the population—or for the Enlightenment's celebration of reason over faith, or for modern atheism, or for selfish individualism that developed at the expense of more generous communal life. Such volumes are balanced by those books that, again not always without foundation, celebrate the Reformation for its contribution to movements of political freedom, as in the Declaration of Independence, or to capitalism, or to sometimes creative sectarian religious divisions.

Notice of these and many more aftereffects overloads the case for the importance of 1517 and its Lutheran "Theses." But the turning-point observation remains credible. In 1983, the five-hundredth anniversary of Luther's birth, some sources reckoned that more books in the Western world had been written about Luther than about anyone else except Abraham Lincoln and Napoleon. It would be hard to define the criteria for measuring this, but that Luther and his work command vast interest is easily observable. By the way, and in passing: repentant commemorators do no one a favor by inflating Martin Luther to superhuman heroic status. He leaves plenty of evidence on thousands of pages in his own vast collection of writings that he was flawed, limited, sinful, often wrong, in need of repentance, and one who had to experience a change of heart. Daily.

Luther had some precedent in his times of church leaders who get dubbed "reformers," figures like Jan Hus in Czech lands, and any number of English Bible translators and reformers. And in Luther's wake, great numbers of "repenters" responded with reform movements, eventually over most of Europe, the West, and in recent centuries well beyond that.

"Oh, come, on," the teacher in me hears a voice say from the back of the class. "All that fuss, pro and con, relates to a parchment four or five pages long, a text once nailed to a church or campus door, a notice of the sort we moderns pass by every day without stopping to look?" To domesticate the heroic story even more, some historians believe the church-door incident is a legend, and contend that Luther started things in an even quieter, less dramatic way. We know that a copy of the Ninety-Five Theses was sent as if by special delivery to the city of Mainz, to a potent superior of young monk Luther, the archbishop of Mainz, an official in the Holy Roman Empire.

A further "Oh, come on!" objection comes from another part of the classroom. We hear someone, or thousands, saying something like, "And so much of all this stir comes down, in the end, to one word or concept, that of repenting or turning or having a change of heart, in the life of a believer? Remember, there are hundreds of important terms that centered events and live on in dictionaries or encyclopedias of philosophy." People who deserve a hearing ask, "Why settle on this unglamorous one?"

# JUSTIFICATION BY FAITH VERSUS THE PENANCE SYSTEM

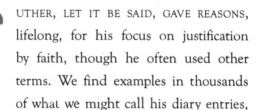

UTHER, LET IT BE SAID, GAVE REASONS, lifelong, for his focus on justification by faith, though he often used other terms. We find examples in thousands of what we might call his diary entries, biblical commentaries, sermons, letters, and debates. All biographies of Luther detail his record of personal agonies over his distance from God and his offenses against God, offenses that could lead to eternal punishment.

The problem to which all of his ninety-five theses related had to do with this focal concept, an obsession of Luther: the biblical claim that one is "made right with God" not through any human effort—the code word then and now was and is "through good works"—but entirely by divine grace "through faith."

Of course, the Catholics also believed in grace and faith. But they disagreed on how grace and faith were effected and experienced and what part the church to which they all belonged was to play. Decisions about all this were desperately urgent, to individuals and to the Christian community, because how one related to these or how these related to anyone determined the fate of believers, all of whom would die and knew they would have to face God the Judge.

In the Catholic understanding, based on some clues in sacred Scripture and developed by theologians of the church, people who died had sinned, and these sins— Scripture said—displeased God the Judge and had to be "purged" before the resurrected person could experience the fullness of divine reward.

"Purged?" Yes, there was in their teachings and grasp a situation and a place of purging called purgatory. It was anything but a pleasant circumstance, but it had to occur in order to help even up the record of the believer and the divine Judge, who had to keep the standards and exact punishment.

The Catholics, terrified by the threat of hell and not cheered by the threat of suffering in purgatory, did believe in a loving and gracious God who, they had to reason, had to make some provision for a happy afterlife. Here is where the system came in: believers could be purged at the time they died and entered the life to come. Their purgation, they were told, lessened the time they had to suffer.

They could have contributed to this minimization already during their earthly years. "Good works" such as fasting, prayer, disciplines, works of love, donations to the church and to needy people, and many more were major contributors. But, after death, a different calculus came into play. Since sinners could no longer contribute to salvation in any direct way, they could identify with and rely on the good works of others. Different teachers in the church determined all this in a variety of ways, but regularly and most notably, particularly virtuous believers—call them saints—had contributed to treasures of God-pleasing works on which one could draw in efforts to please God and shorten or remove the times of purgatorial punishment.

The way to transact this was not simply through repentance and faith in Christ, but had to be supplemented and filled by their acquisition of "indulgences." People who were left behind on earth, then, out of fear for the punishment of others important to them—usually relatives and friends—could make their contribution through the purchasing of these indulgences.

It is not hard to see that such a system appealed to the sympathetic and softhearted, generous people who, readily or resentfully, did without some of their wealth for the sake of those in purgatory. It is also not hard to see that such a system also attracted graft, misrepresentation, and the exploitation of grieving people.

Who profited? Where the system was pure, proceeds went to the purchase of church property or works of charity. Speaking of church property helps us pin down a schedule for measuring corruption around 1517. Roman Catholic authorities were raising funds to build what was and is the largest sanctuary in the Christian world, St. Peter's in Rome.

In Rome! This meant a foreign scene, across the Alps, in domains ruled by princes and bishops who did not represent the people in German lands (or elsewhere beyond Rome). That this part of the system was onerous, irritating, and finally inflaming was to be expected; it is easily documented. As with most bureaucratically inspired ventures, this one attracted specialists to work the system. The most notorious of these was a Dominican priest, Johannes Tetzel, who became "the bad guy" in early Reformation dramas and stories.

Tetzel worked in the German territories, to the profit of his sponsors and himself and at the expense of Germans, who did not like Rome all that much. They may not all have been theologians who had found informed ways to deal with details, but Tetzel and company simply infuriated them. Call their situation one of living in a tinderbox. Then along came a monk who lit the tinder. Debates and demonstrations followed, and the Catholic world was never the same again.

Luther in 1517 had not set out to bait and enrage the pope, but to appraise indulgences and the part they played in purging, but this part was modest compared to what Tetzel and his colleagues were putting to work. There was no mistaking that the Ninety-Five Theses text turned out to be a surprise giant-killer attack on the system. As these were first proposed and delivered, they took the form of a challenge for debates—a rather standard procedure in universities and centers of learning at the time. But these theses got to the point already with the second item. Having praised repentance, Luther took on the term *penance*.

Thesis 2: "The word cannot be understood as referring to the sacrament of penance, that is, confession and satisfaction, as administered by the clergy." Thesis 37 elaborates: "Any true Christian, whether living or dead, participates in all the blessings of Christ and the Church, and this is granted by God, even without letters of indulgence."

Luther also proposed a constructive replacement to the dreaded imposed indulgences. Thesis 45: "Christians should be taught that those who see another in need and pass on by, and then give money for indulgences, are not purchasing for themselves the Pope's indulgences, but rather God's anger." We need quote no more to make clear the case Luther was presenting, and why his understanding of repentance opened the door to fresh ways of thinking with effects on "the entire life of believers." All of such lives should be marked by repentance, the "change of heart."

# CHAPTER five

# FIVE HUNDRED YEARS
# OF CONFLICT

LMOST INSTANTLY GERMAN LANDS AND others in Europe were stirred, and change came on many levels. As events unfolded and more and more Europeans were stunned, challenged, or excited by what the theses invented, extremely complex events followed.

Church reform movements spread, under a variety of leaders. Some of them accented themes similar to those of Luther, while others were quite independent, and owed little more to Luther than an awareness that he had opened the door to change and to their own enterprises and witness. We can speak, for instance, of reform in the Roman Catholic Church, which took the shape of a movement often called the Catholic Reformation.

Across the rivers and, often, mountains to the south, restless and inspired debaters, philosophers, preachers, and social activists in Switzerland promoted distinctive themes. But as far as what came to be called "the Lutheran

Reformation" was concerned, everything came together around a teaching, coded in shorthand: "justification by faith," or, better, "justification by grace through faith."

As we briefly trace the biblical teaching and the Reformation accent, we will see that it fueled many controversies and inspired many sermons, prayers, and actions. One sample of how portable a phrase "justification by faith" can be is the fact that when Communist China set out to abolish all religion, or at least to control expressions of faith and community as far as possible, the Lutheran Church of China became the "Justification-by-Faith Church of Christ." Spiritual heirs of Luther who want to be seen as faithful turn to the biblical letters of Paul the apostle, particularly his Letter to the Romans, where he is explicit about "justification." Most notably, of course, "The righteousness of God is revealed through faith for faith; as it is written, 'The one who is righteous will live by faith'" (Romans 1:17 NRSV).

To report that and to note the claims of loyalty to it is one thing; determining how it works and deservedly is at the heart of Martin Luther and any emphasis close to him is somewhat more difficult. Five hundred years and millions of faithful people later, those who commemorate the turnings of 1517 in many ways do not live in the world people did when the accent developed. Some of these are cultural changes that occurred with historical events. They have an effect on how doctrine is phrased; we shall see evidences of that later in the discussion of Catholic-Protestant conversations and declarations such as the major Catholic-Lutheran Joint Declaration in 1999. I will take one central example, fully aware that there are others bidding for attention by commemorators. This one may well be the biggest inhibitor to understanding the full effect of the Reformation and the joint declaration.

Assigned the task of writing a short biography of Martin Luther some years ago, I had to work through all the metaphors and explanations current at the time Luther wrote. I had to understand both the barrier of the passage of time from 1517 to the twenty-first century and the biblical teachings on which the Reformation and the Catholic-Lutheran Joint Declaration drew. There are many ways to do this, but my readings and observations led me to one of Luther's ways of speaking of justification.

From Luther's first thesis, that Jesus wills that our entire life be one of repentance, his focus connecting the first word, *repentance*, to the formal word *justification* may seem to many of us to be a long stretch. But not to Luther, who saw "repentance" as a "change of heart" from sin to grace, as a joyful act of response to God's activity, a liberating turn. So it is time to talk about this, the heart of Luther's theology.

Readers who picture Luther's theology as being predominantly obscure and abstruse have a surprise coming. While he gave generations to come plenty to read—the latest edition of his works is weighted down in 127 volumes, often in double columns in rather small print—he had many ways to express his thought.

For example, he liked pictures and stories. He came to the publishing scene when movable type was new, books had become more easily available, and some of the major artists of the day were drawn to his gospel preaching. He would see even his earliest printed books brightened with woodcuts, often of biblical scenes. Most significant among these is his seal. For important figures of the day, the etched symbol of its owner told others something about him or her. Picture the typical coat of arms of princes and bishops: many of these suggest noble status, and swords and spears suggest militancy.

Luther was not above resorting to military images. His best-known hymn, a takeoff on Psalm 46, was "A

Mighty Fortress Is Our God." Frederick Hedge's famous, familiar 1852 translation has it as follows:

> A mighty fortress is our God,
> a bulwark never failing;
> our helper he, amid the flood
> of mortal ills prevailing.
> For still our ancient foe
> does seek to work us woe;
> his craft and power are great,
> and armed with cruel hate,
> on earth is not his equal.

But that song talks about God, not about Luther. He made a choice of expression in what today is called "the Luther seal."

Generations of believers schooled in the gospel he proclaimed recognize the Luther seal, often called the Luther rose, from book covers or as rewards on jewelry for well-scored lessons in Sunday schools. Fortunately, we have data that shows why Luther chose the symbols on the seal. Its designer, Lazarus Spengler, who served Prince John Frederick of Saxony, received a letter of July 8, 1530, wherein Luther interpreted the seal. The central and dominant feature, of course, was a heart, but on it was an even more prominent cross, black because the cross "mortifies and . . . should also cause pain." Yet the heart itself, he went on, "retains its natural color," red. Why? "It does not corrupt nature, that is, it does not kill but keeps alive."

Now comes the change of heart. Beyond the black and the red figures is a white rose, "for white is the color of the spirits and the angels (Matthew 28)," according to Luther's interpretation. The white rose is "to show that faith in the crucified gives joy, comfort, and peace." At this point repentance is far from being associated only with self-obsessed gloom. Luther goes on, "Such a rose should stand in a sky-blue field, symbolizing that such joy in spirit and faith is a beginning of the heavenly future joy, which begins already, but is grasped in hope, not yet revealed." Luther rounds things out by describing, surrounding it all, "a golden ring, symbolizing that such blessedness in heaven lasts forever and has no end." It is "exquisite, beyond all joy and goods." Luther called the seal a "compendium" or "summary of theology." In fact, the theology in the 127 volumes is in a way a set of footnotes to the seal.

Note well: nothing in this contradicts the Catholic theology of the day, and is not to be seen as a sign that "there's a war on." The militancy did show its ugly face during countless other "Lutheran" and "Catholic" expressions through the centuries, but common confession, we note, can today exist, and reform can proceed because of this common basis.

Luther proposed his theses and persisted in his program of reform precisely because he thought the Catholic system of penance and the Catholic Church's teaching of the day obscured it. Of course, symbols in print or visually might have dealt with other accents, and through the centuries, many—in "Lutheran" eyes—strayed from and even contradicted elements in the central picture of "Luther's rose" or "Luther's coat of arms."

Hence, the need for a meaningful dialogue in our time.

# REPENTANCE CALLS FOR DIALOGUE, DIALOGUE FOCUSES ON REPENTANCE

IALOGUE ALWAYS IMPLIES AND INVOLVES two or more participants, parties, or partisans. The attention to the heart of Luther and his revolt inevitably evokes more commemoration than does the recall of Catholic response. But the five-hundredth anniversary is not so much a Lutheran story as it is a Catholic-Lutheran or Catholic-Protestant story. And to make sense of the dialogue favored today, we now turn our attention to what this all means for the soul of the Catholic Church.

In an effort to deal freshly with the main themes, as we did by focusing on the key word *repentance* as a "change of heart," we will revisit the key word *Catholic*, referring to the other communion involved. That effort stimulates concentration of the word and concept of "Catholic" and then of its "soul."

*Catholic*, in common discourse in the Western world, refers to the Roman Catholic Church and its cultures. While Catholics, the Orthodox, Lutherans, and other Protestants confess their faith in the "one, holy, catholic, and apostolic church," non-Roman Catholic commentators and revisers of books used in worship often have to insert a footnote or somehow explain that "catholic" belongs to "all of us," and then go on from there. To promote fresh thinking, then, we have to confront convention and cliché alike. In the process we will be better prepared to see why "communion," "community," and ecumenical advances are possible today and tomorrow.

"Catholic" first. On this subject the stimulus for me and many others has come from some etymological work in essays by the late Father Walter Ong, SJ, my main mentor, tutor, and enabler of reconception. While he often took up the concept, nowhere was he more terse and clear than in an article in the Jesuit weekly *America*, on April 7, 1990. There he advocated attention to the Greek words behind "Catholic" rather than to the more restricted base in the Latin word *universalis*. So succinct and clear and decisive (for our purposes) was he, then, that we will listen to him at moderate length.

"Catholic" is commonly said to mean "universal," a term from the Lain *universalis*. The equation is not quite exact. If "universal" is the adequate meaning of "catholic" why did the Latin church, which in its vernacular language had the word *universalis*, not use this word but rather borrowed from Greek the term *katholikos* instead? The etymological history of *universalis* is not in every detail clear; but it certainly involves the concepts of "one," and *vertere*, "turn." It suggests using a compass to make a circle around a central point. It is an inclusive concept in the sense that the circle includes everything within it. But by the same token it also excludes everything outside it. *Universalis* contains a subtle note of negativity. *Katholikos* does not. It is more unequivocally positive. It means simply "through-the-whole" or "throughout-the-whole"—*kata* or *kath*, or through- or throughout-*holos*, whole, from the same Indo-European roots as our English "whole."

Word lovers who focus on this term suggest that the original meaning appears today in combinations like "catholic taste," alluding to a taste that encompasses a wide range of meanings and phenomena.

The Catholicism of Luther's day certainly saw itself as "universal," and documents published in the days of Columbus and Luther claimed the whole world for Catholic power and sovereignty. But in the eyes of Luther and other critics, the "catholic" or "whole" or "holistic" concepts of the faith were being narrowed by practices, definitions, and sovereign or colonial edicts and subsequent corollary practices. The longer career of Luther and the developments of the Catholic Church under the papacy as it faced modernity gave many evidences of further narrowing or fragmenting.

The move toward recovery of the concept of the "whole" came in the twentieth century with the papacy of John XXIII and the Second Vatican Council. It was also based in an impressive devotion to biblical scholarship and the writings of new generations of Catholic theologians. While never a complete realization of wholeness or openness—nothing human ever is— the changes allowed Catholics on all levels, including the highest, to encourage ecumenism, participate in the ecumenical movement, and to be open to new engagement with Protestants and others now often called "separated brothers and sisters." This little book is not a history of that movement and is certainly not a history of modern Catholicism, beyond our focus on the theme of repentance and the "change of heart" toward other Christians. Nevertheless, this change revealed and exposed to view an aspect of Catholicism which we may speak of as its "soul." Little of that could have been visible, encouraged, accessible, or open to engagement and communion had it not been for the evidence and percept of its soul.

At this point, just as we have burnished alternative but appropriate meanings to Luther's call for repentance and the Catholic character of postconciliar Catholicism, we will revisit the meanings of soul. Just as we relied on Walter Ong on "catholic," we'll draw on another scholar, this time Leon Kass, one of my old colleagues from the University of Chicago, a physician, scientist, and educator who gave new, rich, and promising angles of vision on the topic through an essay in his book *Toward a More Natural Science*. Namely, while the Catholic, Lutheran, and larger Christian communities were long familiar with the concept of soul, however elusive its meanings have been, Kass, following Aristotle, made clear that "by soul I mean nothing mystical or religious, not a disembodied spirit or person, not one of Homer's shades or anything else that departs the body intact, not a ghost in a machine or a pilot in a ship, not, indeed a 'thing' at all." Instead, he wrote a paragraph that we'll break down into topical arrangements. Readers may reflect on how these apply—or fail to apply—to the Catholic Church of today. In each case, Kass was referring to an individual human soul, but I take the license of applying it to a corporate body. Thus one notes and can speak of a college or a movement or a nation that embodies "soul." Think of G. K. Chesterton, who once referred to the United States as a "nation with the soul of a church." Here, however, we speak of the Christian church, "the body of Christ," embodying and exemplifying soul, with these features.

Following Kass, then, "soul" is or has (1) the integrated (2) vital (3) powers (4) of a naturally organic body, "always possessed by such a body while it is alive ('animated'). All living things have soul. The ascent of soul has meant the possibility of an ever-greater awareness of and openness to the world and an ever greater freedom in the world." In Kass's view and in my observation, "the hierarchy of soul is a hierarchy of openness and purposiveness."

It was the absence of openness to the gospel, which declares "justification" and purposiveness, in the imperial, legalistic, self-enclosed character of the Catholic

Church of that day, that inspired Luther's reaction and rebellion. Similarly, hierarchical Catholicism saw Lutheran and other Protestant expressions of the church as "closed" from the Catholic Church and influence and lacking the purposes that were supposed to be a part of Christ's church on earth. For all the limits to the ecumenical moves and movement, for all the parts of Christ's body that regard all other parts as sects, be they tiny or massive, still cut-off or cutting-off movements, without doubt, the past century has seen a "change of heart" and a "soul" that is somehow open and purposive. In other words, we've seen a readiness to find new ways for each to regard all the others, and to follow through with action.

# CHAPTER Seven

# ECUMENISTS REPENT:
# THE CHANGE OF HEART

LL THIS BRINGS US TO ONE, BUT BY NO MEANS the only, change: the formal Lutheran-Catholic common moves in the decades leading up to the celebration of the five-hundredth anniversary of Lutheran communal life, and after.

These moves represent a change of heart, born of what I here regard as a synonym, *repentance*. All parties to the dialogue readily admit that their spiritual ancestors grievously offended God, each other, and their neighbors. But the change of heart cannot collapse into a pattern of mutual accusations of their ancestors in the years after 1517 and into the present. The believers of today cannot change the past. They need to be informed about the faults and flaws, the lies and the wars. Learning of this, if it cannot change the past, can at least inform the present. It can open our eyes to history but, again, if it is a correction in vision, it is not by itself a change of heart. So, we look at the record of the past decades and current endeavors to change hearts.

While a billion Roman Catholics and many millions of Lutherans might be expected to have the most at stake in the story of the "changes of heart" that began around 1517, they are not alone in celebrating and commemorating the events of that period or, conversely, in recognizing guilt and repenting for their failures to effect change, or to recognize the need for it. All Christians are somehow affected by their story. Both are leaders in the modern ecumenical movement, and have good reason either to rejoice in gains resulting from dialogue or to be spurred to action in repentance and new interchurch endeavors. They know that people of all Christian communions, from the most staid to the most experimental, constantly live off this story and contribute to it. But they welcome special times to dedicate themselves to the goals of ecumenism, of finding ever more unity in Christ.

High-level agencies and programmers helped set the table for the five-hundredth-year party and its successors. Its title captures both that for which a change of heart is needed and the outcome of the change, in individuals and in churches: *From Conflict to Communion*. Signing on to this product and venture are the Lutheran World Federation (LWF) and the Pontifical Council for Promoting Christian Unity (PCPCU), the duo here having left us in their debt as we leave their acronyms with hints of bureaucracy in the dust. Karlheinz Diez from Fulda, Germany, and Eero Huovinen from Helsinki, Finland, are the main authors. Their foreword begins with a reference to Luther's struggle of 1517 and moves by the third paragraph to what inspires our theme: "Both as individuals and as a community of believers, we all constantly require repentance and reform." They appropriately quote the first of the Ninety-Five Theses, as we've seen, and as I noted in the opening of this little book, to remind us all that "when our Lord and Master Jesus Christ said, 'Repent' (Matthew 4:17), he willed the entire life of believers to be one of repentance."

One paragraph later they get to the point of repentance: that we are to "direct our critical glance first at ourselves and not at each other." They soon shift their focus to the *Joint Declaration on the Doctrine of Justification*. Is not this title a sign that the Catholics granted the basic framework in the endeavor to the Lutherans, heirs of the man who so offended Catholics five centuries ago and, as until recently many Catholics would add, has ever since?

Some Catholics faulted the "pontifical" participants for having given too much away, saying they were focusing on Luther's definition of the focus of revolt and reform. And some Lutherans were likewise suspicious of their own spokespeople: How could they get Catholics to experience such a drastic change of heart after centuries of conflict?

But the authors were trading on a half century of changed-heart-and-mind actions as part of their life in the ecumenical age. Rather than shrink from their task because we live in a global scene that is both secular and pluralist, they welcomed the occasion as an agent to provoke new witness to Jesus Christ and God's act of justifying sinners. They recognized that many kinds of active Christians on the global scene do not use or need those "-ation" ending words like "justification," but rather than losing heart, they accepted the burden of finding terms and situations that will help draw many other believers—they name, among others, the Pentecostal millions—to draw further on biblical witness to God's gracious action.

Today, Catholics and Lutherans and others credit twentieth-century Catholic research on Luther as a boon. They tell of the ways Catholic scholars in that century came to appreciate Luther in new ways and could see Martin Luther and Thomas Aquinas, the magisterial Catholic theologian, as sharing many concerns that had been lost in the period of mere conflict. They also show how the Second Vatican Council let Catholicism be more freely Catholic, in the terms we borrowed from Walter Ong: it can now deal with "the whole" as never before, and thus be open to new possibilities. They cite both Pope John Paul II and Benedict XVI, neither ever seen as "liberal" compromisers, as discoverers of new paths toward unity.

It is not and cannot be our purpose to revisit all the themes in the pages of *From Conflict to Communion*, which I commend to all. Nor is it possible to retrace all the history behind and during the indulgence controversy that raged in the decades of Luther's theses and beyond. Suffice it here simply for us to remind ourselves that indulgences, peddled, purchased, and misused, provoked Luther's cry in thesis number one for repentance, the change of heart that allowed the gospel to be realized among believers. We should also recognize that the response to all of the theses, and to Luther's provocations generally, was surprising even to Luther, not to mention to his colleagues. We also recognize that these debates quickly forced new probings of Scripture, which were quickly perceived as assaults on papal authority.

As the conflicts continued, it became clear that arguments over justification by faith could not be isolated and contained. How to read the Bible, how to govern the church, how to deal with earthly authority, how to live the Christian life, how to confess sins, seek the moral life, receive the sacraments, and more, became a complex that set all Christians, at first in Europe, on a new course. Since every part of this complex led to conflict, all parts of what came from Luther's heart and lived in the Catholic soul forced or induced or inspired Catholic, Lutheran, and other Christians to seek "communion" in new ways. If the entire Christian life is to be one of repentance—a change of heart—questions remain about how this repentance reaches each Christian. Somehow we have to learn from and move beyond *From Conflict to Communion*. We can do this by reflecting on the genre, the character of expression, and the concerns within documents like this.

I can perhaps illustrate this best by reference to a typical commissioned and bureaucratically generated document that has had much consequence in ecumenical discussions. Called the New Delhi Statement on Unity (1961), it witnesses to the belief that "all in each place who are baptized into Jesus Christ and confess him as Lord and Saviour are brought by the Holy Spirit, into one fully committed fellowship."

This was an astonishing signal of "repentance" for the bitter sectarian divisions in the church. Yet I recall the musings in the press room at a subsequent ecumenical forum where the document handed out perhaps reflected the reflexive typing of a servant of an ecumenical bureaucracy. This ephemeral—indeed, quickly disposed of—page transposed the phrase "fully committed fellowship" to a "full committee fellowship"!

Perhaps most Christians who hear of ecumenical documents produced in committees and commissions, regard them, if they know of or pay attention to them at all, as unrepresentative statements, far removed from the lived life of most Christians. They dismiss them as jargon-filled, precious, and remote documents with which they do not have to contend.

Yet, from another angle, they are wrong. One thinks, for example, of the influence of those already-mentioned schemata of the Second Vatican Council in the Catholic

Church or the many Protestant-grounded documents that reach into and speak for members of the churches, often called "the laity," who are not ordained to the office of ministry. As a Lutheran, I think of the impact of Lutheran documents that, after four centuries, compel witness to the strong anti-Semitism in so much of Lutheran church life, and what a drastic change of heart and mind in this field have meant in recent decades. Similar confessions of sins in relations among races within the churches witness to what has been wrong—and call for newness of life.

If a document like *From Conflict to Communion* is to be a part of a life of repentance and a change of hearts, we do well also to think of what a response to it cannot easily produce. Such agreement cannot, for instance, reflect the way that divisions within the Christian church touch, color, shadow, and limit the lives of believers.

We might welcome a close-up. Picture a newly married couple who are also new to Christian faith and are participating in a Lutheran or a Catholic parish. The two are confronted by news of a commemoration like this one and by literature calling them to repent, to have a change of heart. During the seasons leading up to their marriage, they have likely examined their ways more intentionally than they have at any other time. As they embark on marriage, if they are serious people, they no doubt talk a good deal about their guilt and their hopes.

What is their new agenda? We can picture that they know they must change from the ways that have led to past broken relationships, to new tensions over the attitudes of some in-laws, to weaknesses of which they are both all too aware. Now, with their fresh alliances, the calls come: "Repent over the divisions that separate Christians! Ask for a change of heart, because the actions of your hearts contribute to church division!" A suggestion: hand them *From Conflict to Communion*, and ask them to start there.

The path to this moment took a major turn in the Second Vatican Council (1962–65), when its episcopal participants and their theologians and pastors reviewed the history surrounding 1517 and leading up to the Catholic-Lutheran Joint Declaration in 1999. In more recent times, especially at and after the council, the "openness" of the Catholic soul became manifest in many actions and documents that cheered non-Catholic observers and reporters (I, among them, covering the third autumnal session). In 1964 in *Lumen Gentium*, the bishops spoke of the fact that outside the structures of the Catholic Church "many elements of sanctification and of truth" were found as gifts of the church of Christ that impelled all Christians toward unity. This countered the main thrust of a papal document of 1943, which had neglected to mention and even closed off all non-Catholics from the recognition of these gifts. Now in 1964, several other approved and disseminated documents explicitly called for change of heart and repentance for past injuries inflicted by Christians against other Christians, or to the whole body of Christ.

Would the language of the bishops in council and linked to papal authority seem remote to many? Particularly, why would Catholics or other Christians who had had no part in the formulation of principles and practices that were now being redefined and in effect replaced feel involved? Wouldn't it be most likely that people we might call "ordinary Christians" would not recognize any part they have had in these church divisions? They had not even been of "the church." Where, our couple would surely wonder, does such a concern come from?

Now they are participating in the sacrament of the Lord's Supper or Communion for the first time. Suppose one of them had been denied a place at the table. They have to ask: what did they do to lead those who preside at Communion to deny the bread and wine to one of them?

Or, if they have been communicants, but in separate communions, why can they not come together now? The most immediate place where all this is felt is in what are called "mixed marriages." Some of these differences look trivial on a global ecumenical scale, but they are burdensome and limiting. The marriages of two members of separate and long-warring Protestant communions are examples. These can result in misunderstanding and conflict. Often the differences are based in ignorance of "the other," differences that can be overcome by education and counseling.

Far more difficult are the differences to which this quincentenary project is directed. When theological, canonical (law), and especially sacramental issues are the focus of conflict, much more is demanded of all parties. But for now we need to mainly recognize the searingly painful up-close marital and familial conflicts this side of communion can be. Any adequate address to these, even if partial and faltering, can contribute to the rewarding Christian life of individuals and families.

Along the way, we can be inspired by what steps short of dogmatic and legal change and full ecumenical communion can achieve in reaching the hearts of believers. On Martin Luther's five-hundredth birthday in 1983, the Catholic archbishop of Chicago, Cardinal Joseph Bernardin invited congregants from the four-hundred-plus Lutheran parishes in greater Chicago to observe the event together. Invited to preach, I scanned the crowd before entering the pulpit, expecting to see four-hundred-plus or more people wearing clerical collars. Yet the majority were dressed in the going-to-church apparel of laypeople. After the service, stepping into the clergy receiving line to which preachers and assistants are accustomed, I was treated courteously but was largely irrelevant. Instead, I witnessed one or two couples from most parishes, in each case one being Catholic and one being Lutheran. We saw many tears of joy and heard many testimonies about how refreshing the invitation and service had been: here, for the first time, sometimes after decades of marriage, the husband and wife were both recognized as Christians in a sanctuary. Many told how they were not allowed to be present at their own children's baptisms or other sacramental rites—though many all but winked as they told the cardinal how they had cheated by worshiping together. If I shed tears, it was because of what the very limited nonsacramental joint life still meant, and recognized new resolve to work for "communion."

One thing more is to be said as we discuss the values and limits of "full committee fellowship" of commission-based advances. The scholars, many of them clergy, alone and in company, are imperfect. They are schooled in hermeneutics, the "science of interpretation," which recognizes that all interpretation is colored by the prejudgments, experiences, ideals—I don't want to say ideologies—and outlooks they bring. In this way, profoundly informed Catholics from India will sound different from their counterparts in Poland; and, similarly, Lutherans from South Africa have had different church experiences from those in North America. That so many of them can agree on so much after so long is a testimony to the power of their efforts and, I am sure all would say, of the Holy Spirit. So, differences remain.

One more illustration, discussed in *From Conflict to Communion*, was evident especially among Lutherans in 1999. That year the joint commission issued a joint declaration on justification by faith. This common witness or doctrine or teaching was, by common agreement, the sticking point, stumbling block, or inflaming issue whenever 1517 and its churchly consequences were brought up. It still awakens some awe and maybe a regard for the miraculous that the pontifical council agreed to deal with "justification" as the point of contention, the problem of differences over which—and the way they were lived out—was the main issue, page one.

The Catholics signed on, as did the Lutherans. No doubt there were Catholics "back home" who were miffed that justification was recognized as determinative and that their leaders were now recognizing their part in conflicts that issued from the Ninety-Five Theses and kin documents. But, perhaps to no one's surprise, some Lutherans, especially from Germany, Hungary, and some circles in the United States, reacted strenuously.

It is important to recall what *had* occurred. For the first time in five hundred years, in a drastic act, the Catholic Church officially revoked its formal condemnation of Luther and what he represented. There was now an open and acknowledged repentance, a change of heart, and mind. Church bodies through their leaders don't often say publicly, "We were wrong," or "We didn't understand you back then," or "We had to go back to Scripture and ahead to the needs of the future church to get to where we are on the ecumenical pilgrimage." Now their actions showed that they were confessing that their old ways impeded the efforts of Christians to realize the "one, holy, catholic, and apostolic church."

As the Lutheran critics picked at fine points of disagreement and connected them to legitimate concerns over justification—and let me intrude by saying that I have some agreements with some of their disagreements—to the point that they wanted to reject the historic agreement, the hearts of many fell. My own perspective came from a story Winston Churchill used to recount. In Churchill's telling, a British family, picnicking near a lake, saw their five-year-old tumble in and submerge to the point that he might drown. No one in the immediate company knew how to swim, but a passerby who did, though clothed and at risk to himself, dove in and reached the child just before he went under for the third time. The swimmer finally presented the child to his mother, who then, instead of thanking him for his sacrificial and heroic act, snapped, "Where's Johnny's cap?"

Now, I realize that much of what I've written in this chapter deals with documents that too few have had reason to read, but which many, when informed of their existence, might then feel a need to take up and consider. For that reason, a final story will help me put in perspective the genre of the document-based ecumenical change.

This tale concerns a man who was tarred and feathered and seen to be running for his life at the edge of a village on a summer night. He collapsed into the arms of rescuers who asked him what had been at issue, what had fired up the mob to torture him. He answered: "The Monroe Doctrine." A bit bemused by this contention on a summer evening, one asked, "Why were they so angry and stirred up?" He said, "I told them, 'I believe in the Monroe Doctrine. I live by the Monroe Doctrine. I'd die for the Monroe Doctrine. I just told them that I didn't know what was in it.'"

# chapter eight

# FROM MERE DIVERSITY TO RECONCILED DIVERSITY

K NOWING WHAT IS IN A DOCUMENT IS BOTH easier and more difficult than it was five hundred years ago. Late twentieth-century Lutheran-Catholic and larger ecumenical statements and moves appeared not in a simple culture of homogeneity, but one of great diversity within and around the church. Five hundred years ago, there was diversity among the people, even though most were Christian and rarely met anyone from a culture that did not have a Christian lineage. In contrast today, five hundred years later, to speak of religion without reckoning with diversity and pluralism is very limiting. Historians, social scientists, demographic experts, as well as anyone professionally involved in matters of religion have to deal with great variety. We are told, for instance, that there are now some forty thousand Christian denominations in the world. Part of Luther's legacy.

The Catholic Church in the sixteenth century was just beginning to come into contact with the religions of China and India, and was being forced to deal with the Islamic world in a new way. Martin Luther had his hands and eyes full without looking to the New World or much of anywhere else. The two primary non-Christian religious peoples with which they had to deal were Jews and Muslims, but they were not organizationally connected to Western Christianity.

In a bracing comment, the British philosopher Alfred North Whitehead once highlighted the smallness of the world in which these various sixteenth-century reformations occurred. He and others pointed to how modern science was intruding on and challenging traditional Christianity. For the most part, dealing with the emerging scientific worldview was still the task of specialists. Islam was expanding, reaching into Europe, and the Reformers were well aware that "the Turk" who conquered Constantinople in 1453 was now on the verge of attacking Vienna. Still, the thought of the Muslim world, important in the sciences and competitive exploration, hardly shows up in Reformation talk.

Within the world of religions, Whitehead spoke of the Reformation as a family quarrel of northwest

European peoples. Even Christians of the East, in Orthodoxy, "serenely ignored" what was going on between giant Rome and upstart Wittenberg and the states, cities, and churches of Western Europe. All those changes were impending, or could still be treated as side issues. While there was considerable internal variety in the Catholic world and increasing diversity within the realms of the Reformers, in the story of the Reformation two main forces contended fatefully. The concentration on Luther and the emerging Protestants on the Continent and in the British Isles is well-placed.

If 1517 symbolizes the great breach within Western Christianity, any efforts to repair it merit attention.

While wars, enmities, and defamations of "the other" dominated for more than four centuries, thoughtful Christians were aware that they were living a lie or revealing a weakened conscience whenever in their creeds they said that they believed in "one, holy, catholic, and apostolic church" but did nothing to see that faith realized. Doing anything about it must have seemed almost impossible, since the destinies of Reformation Christianity and Catholicism were so tied into accepted patterns of commerce, nationhood, and culture that it was hard to know where to start to realize anything about the "oneness" of the church.

Most Christians, it is safe to suggest, were unaware of or paid little attention to the event in 1999 signaled by the issuance of *The Joint Declaration on the Doctrine of Justification*. For that matter, most Catholics and Lutherans, however they had acted toward each other, and regardless of how eager they were for Christian unity, may not have gone about their business and their lives of faith any differently because commissions far from their shores or the scope of their denominational magazines announced a declaration.

Television newscasters had not exactly gotten into the habit of starting programs with announcements such as, "Breaking News: Lutherans and Catholics Are on a New Course." Responsible leaders in the churches did their best to publicize the event and to guide members to join celebrations, but events like this do not seem urgent on the secular news front the way headlines such as "Lutherans Approve Gay Marriage" or "Election of a New Pope" are noticed.

One main reason for any stir was the words "Doctrine of Justification" in the program of the goings-on. Scholars and clerics had not spent the half century on issues such as "Churches Sharing Parking Lots in Crowded Downtowns," or should they celebrate the Festival of the Transfiguration of Christ on the Sunday after Epiphany or on August 6. They did not thumb through old seminary library books and scan an alphabet of doctrines until they came to "J" and, along the way, "Justification." No, both groups knew it was central, the nagging and burdening issue that seemed to be treated as if they occupied different islands. But even if most Christians in the larger culture may not have noticed, Lutherans and Catholics could not advance without confronting the issue that divided and shadowed their relations for almost five centuries; the heart of Lutheran witness: justification by faith.

# CHAPTER nine

# RECONCILED DIVERSITY OVER "JUSTIFICATION"

OR THEIR PART, CATHOLICS WOULD NOT have located "justification" at the heart and center of their church, as Lutherans did when they looked at or thought about the meaning of the white cross on the black heart on the Luther seal. Lutherans did locate the term, the doctrine, the issue, at their heart because it was a code name for the complex things that Luther and other Reformers thought mattered most and best defined their differences. Their early Augsburg Confession (1530) defined justification as "the article [doctrine] by which the church stands or falls."

Catholics and Lutherans in the twentieth century knew how far their ancestors for five centuries after 1517 had to reach to make their point. They could have found in formal language that the Catholic Church had issued a "doctrinal condemnation" against Lutherans and their version of justification. You do not lightly flip away such a drastic judgment, nor do you bypass it in efforts to be nice and agreeable. Sooner or later, and definitely sooner in church relations, both and all parties will find it impossible to ignore the impassible route toward unity or reunion.

Aware of their need both to advance toward Christian unity and to do justice to the values nurtured by the separate churches without completely altering every detail of their legacies, they sought new patterns and new terms to define them. One of the most widely accepted approaches was condensed in a phrase issued by the World Council of Churches in 1984: "reconciled diversity." This phrase seemed to sum up the most positive approach at the time, and it was in this spirit that the Catholics and Lutherans were ready to move toward their great statement of 1999 on justification. Most Lutheran bodies around the world saw this as a charter for going deeper in the search for Christian unity. How about the Catholics?

For Lutherans, with their many churches, whether in the "Federation" or not, there was no simple mechanism that could represent all. Catholicism offered a different kind of face and lived with a different structure. To put it simply, its unity and its policies in the end, and often long before that, were defined by the pope—though after the Second Vatican Council it was stated that papal authority was exerted "collegially," in the company of the bishops. The arrangement was clear, though of course it did not solve all of the issues. One could put it this way: papal authority does not always assure the way for the church to step forward, but without it, not much can happen.

Stepping back, in the Week of Prayer for Christian Unity in January 1959, Pope John XXIII reached out to the "separated communities" to "seek again" the unity long disrupted. John's successor Pope Paul VI followed his example and welcomed Protestant and Orthodox official visitors to the Second Vatican Council. Some formal statements of the bishops in council documents pushed for ecumenical efforts, signaling that a new age was being realized. To the point of our story, at the end of the council, in 1965, the Catholic Church and the Lutheran World Federation authorized a working group to advance unity moves.

Major Catholic theologians followed through by reaching into theological resources and locating the barriers and problems. They came, again and again, to the issue of justification by faith. How could the two

Christian entities overcome their own pasts to view the other and the path to unity in a new way? Catholics stressed the role of human effort in cooperation with the Holy Spirit to realize different levels and stages of grace. Lutherans, upon hearing of "efforts" or "works" or "cooperation," were suspicious of and opposed to such approaches. For them, the whole process of justification was marked by divine grace. Luther was so emphatic about this that when he translated the Bible, he had even—scandalously, in Catholic eyes—inserted the word "alone," as in "faith alone," into Romans 1:17 (quoted above from the New Revised Standard Version) even though it was not there in the original Greek text.

How did Lutherans differ? For the moment, we have to introduce a Latin phrase, because it conveniently sums up everything, and is translatable and portable. So profound is the Lutheran commitment to what it stands for that after 1999 some protesting Lutherans claimed that it was being obscured. Here it is: the repenting human is still *simul justus et peccator*, "at the same time" made "just" as she remains a "sinner." Conceiving of the human being in this way left nothing but God's gracious activity in the sacrifice of Christ, to which the sinner responds in faith—again, this time, faith *alone*.

While we have the Latin dictionary out, we spy the term for the Christian's relation to God: *sola fide*, by faith alone.

From the beginning, when dialogues began, it became clear that, so long as Catholics spoke to Catholics about the Lutherans, and Lutherans spoke to Lutherans about the Catholics, they were free to do what people in close groups often do: they could "invent the other," and assign all kinds of strange interpretations to them. Often these acts of assigning were part of virtual (and sometimes even actual) holy wars, as European history for four centuries and more revealed. Just as often, however, with all goodwill and scholarly passion, they still were misrepresenting the other. When dialogue (dia+logue) began, each could hear the other, and they held more accurate views across the church boundaries.

Thus, while Lutherans heard Catholics "mixing" grace and "works," they concluded that Catholics were compromising the reality of the grace of God. They undervalued the countless ways in which Catholics through the ages, through liturgies and chants and prayers, were celebrating grace. It was not a time in which they were eager to hear from Catholics how they worked this out. And while Catholics heard Lutherans celebrating "grace," which is generally music to Catholic ears, they nevertheless heard attacks on "works" that seemed to witness to a God who was capricious, who did not honor the good to which Jesus commended them, and left the believers passive. No, said Lutherans in dialogue: watch us and listen to us: we celebrate human participation, but we want to see "works" as a consequence of belief in the works of God through believing humans and not a contributor to salvation itself, in which God is the sole agent.

Both sides had a long way to go, but as is the case in dialogue or conversation, one understanding leads to another to everyone's profit. By 1972 the conversation partners were ready to announce in a "Malta Report" that "a far-reaching consensus was developing in the interpretation of justification." In our terms, "consensus" meant that in Christian witness, the heart of Luther's teaching reflected an understanding of aspects of the soul of Catholicism.

But then, neither party could be content with their hearings and speeches of 1972. In 1980, during a celebration of the 450th anniversary of the Lutheran Augsburg Confession, the participants reached a new consensus that "it is solely by grace and by faith in

Christ's saving work and not because of any merit in us that we are accepted by God and receive the Holy Spirit who renews our heart and equips us for and calls us to good works."

The first half of that phrase sounded so congenial to Lutherans and other Protestants, on the one hand, that some said it was a "burying of the hatchet" between the two parties, with some Lutherans even claiming that it was a Catholic surrender. Some Catholics, on the other hand, heard that phrase "good works" sneaking in or peeking through a Lutheran statement, and it sounded to them, too, like a surrender from the other side. Not so fast, said the participants in the dialogue, who pointed out that there was much work to be done; that not all was settled. Still, more had been accomplished in respect to this one, central doctrine by these representative bodies in one decade than had been effected in the 450 years prior to it. It was time for a public joint declaration, which was prepared over the next twenty years.

After much refinement and clarifying with the faithful back home, the leaders of the Lutheran World Federation and the Pontifical Council for Promoting Christian Unity were ready to present for passage and declaration the *Joint Declaration on the Doctrine of Justification*. Famously, as we have noted, some Lutheran theologians responded very negatively, in documents that received wide publicity. Nevertheless, these negative responses did not deprive most Catholics, Lutherans, and other Protestants of the impulse and means to continue repenting, experiencing a change of heart after half a millennium of consistent nonrecognition of the other, of brother and sister fellow Christians.

To say that churches dealt with the central issue does not mean that everything connected with it has been addressed. In many respects, the half century of dialogues took the form of, and could be perceived as, an intellectual venture of scholarly experts. But rather than constantly picking over what had been declared, Catholics and Lutherans in their homes, parishes, social action, seminaries, and gatherings have the opportunity to newly treat practices and teachings that still separate them and prevent the unitive commands, promises, and practices from being further developed. We shall explore some of these.

# SACRAMENTS AND PRACTICES AMONG REPENTANT CHRISTIANS

W HEN LUTHERANS AND CATHOLICS entered dialogues, both discerned strengths and weaknesses in the inherited life and practice of their own body and in that of the other. Catholics acknowledged that they had much to learn to respond to the biblical witness to the Word, which, say Lutherans, is what combines with the application of water to amount to baptism. Karl Rahner, the most notable senior Catholic theologian of the period, contributed most to fresh understandings, and wrote things pleasing to Lutheran theologians of the Word when he called the Word "the essence of the sacrament," which the visible element, water, reinforces. Lutherans acknowledged that Catholic faith and practice more vividly offered reinforcement of a symbolic character.

In a work critical of Catholic teaching, Luther did not attack its versions of witness to baptism. Luther contributed by accenting the role of baptism as an aid in *daily* life. In his *Large Catechism* he had called baptism "a daily dying to sin and rising to new life. Thus it is a continuing call to repentance, faith, and obedience to Christ." Catholic teaching has differed somewhat in how all this is effected, but the two churches came to agreement on the final result in "repentance, faith, and obedience." Lutherans have come to recognize more than before what Catholics stress: that baptism makes one an organic member of a community, *the community* that is the body of Christ. Both churches baptize infants, and do not rebaptize anyone baptized with water and the Word of God. So baptism is permanent; one may fall away from the life in baptism, but repentance and return remain possible and are received as divine gifts. The Catholic belief in the sacrament of penance leads to a somewhat more complex churchly involvement in this return, but there is more agreement than disagreement on all this.

The Eucharist, or Communion or the Lord's Supper, is a very different matter and a greater problem in ecumenical relations. No one pretends that affairs are the same in this second sacrament in the Lutheran counting and the second of seven in the Catholic. Disagreements over the meaning of the Eucharist have plagued Lutherans within Protestantism from the beginning, and most Protestant ecumenical effort stumbles here first. Luther's view that "in, with, and under" the bread and the wine in Communion, the believer receives Christ in his "real presence" was not acceptable to many other kinds of Protestants, who tended to regard the bread and wine as symbols of Christ's presence. How Protestants address this is urgent for their uniting future, but is not central to the Lutheran-Catholic discussion. In dialogue one will sometimes hear the Catholic participants saying that the Lutheran formula is, if anything, more direct than that of the Catholic, which has long transacted philosophically with forbidding-sounding words such as *transubstantiation*. The final two syllables in such words, *-ation*, signal a philosophical complication that makes it more difficult to connect with the simplicity of Jesus's words spoken in the Upper Room, according to the Gospel: "This . . . my body," in Aramaic, Jesus's spoken language, or "This *is* my body," in the translations and interpretations that Lutherans and Catholics stress.

If there is agreement on the "real presence of Christ" in the Eucharist, by no means is everything settled, since *how* he is present is explained differently among the faithful. For this reason, this has become the most pressing item in the "not yet fulfilled" list in the agendas. The meaning of these differences is clear to the Mass-goer whenever one is denied access to the sacrament at the altar of the other communion. Many who preside at the Eucharist, aware of this, sometimes treat it pastorally, and allow for openness at the Table, but they do not relish such a role and sometimes have some explaining to do when accosted about their irregular action. One will see wringing of hands among ecumenically minded priests and teachers at this point, and tears are often visible.

Equally vivid in the category of "we still have a long way to go on the path to unity" is Luther's primal revolt against the Catholic understanding of the Mass as a sacrifice, an heir of ancient Israel's commended rite to sacrifice an animal to draw God's favor. Luther also believed that the gifts of money or property and other penitential practices negated the reality that God's grace in the sacrament of the Eucharist does all the work, and that the communicant is a recipient. While modern Catholic rituals, more than before, stress the grace-full character of what happens in the Eucharist and Lutheran congregants more readily than before acknowledge that believing congregants bring *something* to the Mass, both sides are trying to clarify their beliefs, intentions, and witness in ways that show them to be closer to the other as both are drawn more closely to God in Jesus Christ. One can also "see" a difference in that Catholics regarding the sacramental presence of Christ in the host, or bread, as continuing after the Mass, whereas Lutherans, respectful though they may be regarding the bread and wine, regard them after the sacramental observance, to be "ordinary." They are still reserved about or critical of Catholic "adoration" of Christ in the form of his body in the bread and wine.

One more clearly defined remaining difference on the Eucharist is a matter of auspices, which is far from resolved. Catholics believe that only ordained priests in the "apostolic succession" can preside at the Eucharist and, without that instrumentality, the observance is not a true Eucharist at all. Lutherans are very careful about the auspices in sacramental observance, and most of their bodies have elaborate safeguards against presiding by others than those ordained to the *office* of Word and sacrament. But the Catholic understanding of apostolic succession and ordination differs from the Lutheran and all Protestant versions. No one pretends that differences over this are resolved.

That irresolution signals another major hurdle in Lutheran-Catholic relations and one more opportunity for very practical grappling on the ecumenical-dialogue front: the office of ministry, the meaning of "ordination" to the office of ministry, and more. The accent on the "office" derives from Luther and his heirs. They regard all people of faith grafted into the body of Christ by baptism as "ordained," but not to this office.

Differences remain unresolved in the matter of women's roles, especially with respect to their ordination. Until recent decades, Lutherans did not ordain women. But in the late twentieth century, beginning in Western Europe, then in North America, and ever since throughout the rest of the globe, they began to appear in the priesthood of the Episcopal Church and then in Lutheranism— where the category "priest" is less frequently employed. The motives for this "change of heart," repentance for past attitudes and actions that at worst demeaned women and, more positively, undervalued them in the offices and the life of the church, are many. Of course, the main impetus came from women, some of them inspired by what some called "secular" movements. Not all of these changes came about singularly from gender issues, but were part of broader concerns for equal rights and justice.

Catholicism had lore and treasures on which to draw to suggest that, within certain limits, women not only have been honored but have also been fervent activists and exemplars. Catholic devotion to Mary as the Mother of God reveals that they do not undervalue women, and the roster of women in the calendar of saints underscores this. Many of the vocations of saints have specifically related to women and their roles in the life of the church. As far as womanpower in the church is concerned, orders of nuns, sisters, deaconesses, and the like make their point by their presence and activities. Classical, canonical, and traditional interpretations of womanhood—that, for instance, they did not bear a likeness to Christ—has kept them excluded from being considered for ordination.

Catholic women in movements in many nations, however, have made declarations that state their case more boldly. Such outspoken women make clear that change will come only through acts of repentance, over where the whole church has failed women, and it has become common to urge a change of heart by way of envisioning their case biblically. For a Lutheran male to state the case further would be unbecoming and ineffective; I can testify, however, to the power of the pool of talent, the human resources on display, and the theological acumen of Catholic women who urge repentance over the past, which suggests promising future developments.

As for ordination in general, not a few observers note that among Lutherans there have been fierce debates over ordination, not only of women but also of gays and others who do not meet traditional qualifications. Observers press debaters to find definitions of ordination because, as the record makes clear, Luther and the Lutherans did not have a clear delineation of the meanings of ordination.

This does not mean that Lutherans have traditionally had no sense of ordered ministry: northern Europeans were classically "ordered" and "ordering" people. They simply could not find a biblically prescriptive command or definition, and they insist the there must be such to make a practice a stipulated and regulated ordinance. Meanwhile, these Protestants, especially Episcopalians and Lutherans, have shown respect for the priesthood, especially since the Second Vatican Council, which in the eyes of most put ever greater accent on the part the Word of God played in the concepts and actions of ministry. Even the revision in liturgy and the placement of the altar, which posts the priest to face the people, has been an important symbol of change. Lutherans find this congenial, because in their tradition after 1520 Luther began to preach about the "universal priesthood of all believers."

Who is authorized to administer the sacraments? Differences on this, questions about the credentials, and competences of leaders across the confessional divide are more visible to most believers than are the documents on justification. What are the impulses that lead Christians to respond to God's call to discipleship and the service of the neighbor? Catholic and Protestant agencies often outpace secular organizations, but they do not always get to serve together. These and other fronts, when mentioned, illustrate how far Christians have to go to realize the unity in Christ they profess to have been promised. For all these reasons, the commemorations in and after the five-hundredth year since the Ninety-Five Theses call for and will receive more attention than anything else in the effort to see what all was involved after churches recognize what is the heart, or is *in* the heart, of Lutheranism and what can change the world through the understandings and work of the Catholic soul.

# eleven

## CAN ONE DAY CHANGE THE WORLD?

THE BOLD CLAIM IN THE SUBTITLE OF this book is that October 31, 1517, is the day that changed the world. Questions come to mind when one reads such an assertion. Do days change the world? Do days do anything? Don't people and natural forces such as hurricanes do the changing on particular days? If there is such world-changing, who decides which day matters? Why focus on a day when events of a particular day are related to days both before and after?

On second thought, there is likely some wisdom in loading up the case for a particular day. Private individuals are likely to admit that *their* world changed when, for example, they married, or received a diagnosis of terminal cancer. Most groups and movements single out particular days as world-changing for each of them. The claim is, of course, more difficult to make, the larger the scene. Topple a regime in a Latin American nation or one in Southeast Asia, and, while a story about it makes the news, life goes on in most of the rest of the world as it was going on before. Still, some particular events of *a* day, *the* day, can have a double consequence, altering those immediately involved at once but then having a ripple effect that sustains or magnifies the decisive change.

Before setting out to make the case for the "world-changing" date October 31, 1517, it helps to return to our earlier comparison. July 4, 1776, was big news in Philadelphia and then in thirteen British colonies that were on that day chartered to invent a new nation. Of course, there were lead-ups to it, in actions of restless colonists, in the British and colonial American philosophies and theologies that envisioned a polity for free people. And then the "changed world" had continuing effects globally, as America came to power and, through its markets and outlets, effected change all over the globe.

Some dates change the world as people respond to disasters or threats. Certainly what is coded as "9/11" altered the world of Americans and also affected citizenries that found themselves less secure ever after.

December 7, 1941, "Pearl Harbor," was world-changing, as an actual and symbolic date for America's involvement in, yes, the Second *World* War. Its date cannot be isolated from "before" and "after" images and experiences of a world, *the world*.

So far, so good. Now we zero in on a day in which a youngish monk of whom very few had heard, in a province that did not matter much to inhabitants of provinces far away, took action that in ordinary circumstances would have riled a little university campus—can we even call it by such a pretentious-sounding name?—in Saxony, which was far away from most centers of influence and power. And think of his obscure issue! It had to do with God, the Invisible about whom mortals argued without resolution, a portion of the church, one of its rites (confession and penance), and what looks from a distance like a nuance, a subtlety about repenting. So what? Whether one should "confess" through a penance system or whether one should let or cause "repentance" to be the focus of life every day. Does it matter? Yet that call to repentance is what happened in an apparently overlookable day, October 31, 1517.

That this monk, Martin Luther, acted in the context of long-term debates about whether God is gracious, and whether God's grace changes the world, *our* world, leads October 31, 1517, to be regarded as a day of decision. Luther was not the first to question the system in which agents of the church controlled penance, remission, forgiveness, and, yes, access to eternal life. And to enlarge on the claim in the subtitle, there have to be aftereffects that continue into today's world. Historians, year in and year out, especially in special years when anniversaries of October 31, 1517, are commemorated, are busy measuring both the power and the limits of what that day symbolizes.

From many distances, both the world of Martin Luther and that of the guardians of the Catholic soul are remote and almost meaningless. Most people in the worlds shaped and dominated by Hinduism, Buddhism, animism, and other "isms" pay little attention to old events involving "the heart of Martin Luther and the soul of the Catholic church." As I mentioned earlier, quoting philosopher Alfred North Whitehead, Eastern Christians "serenely ignored" what came to be called "the Reformation." Even in the historical "heartland" of European and Western Christianity, generations by design or changing their practice, join the "serenely ignoring" club.

Such reducing, however, misses much in the larger world and closer to the homes and hearts of millions. Secular commentators in Luther-anniversary years often make much of Luther's contribution to the spread of human liberty beyond the world of church and spirituality. The cultural contributions after October 31, 1517, are also vast. Thus it happens that Luther himself had a passionate interest in music, and encouraged the participation of musicians both in the church and outside of it. People in his tradition also had great impact on law. For one example, Luther advocated "secularized" approaches to marriage law and saw marriage as an issue for the state. It may be blessed by the church, but the state "regulates" it. While what Americans call "the separation of church and state" is grounded in later philosophies— Luther certainly did not invent it—his vision of God's "two kingdoms," one an "earthly realm" and the other dealing with eternal life, had an influence on many aspects of life in the church-and-state realms. Yes, this date "changed" the world.

Still, faithfulness to the record leads to a more modest and chastening claim: Luther's initiative in 1517 and before and after reveals him to have been, to use a word coined beyond his realm, "God-intoxicated," with a theology always centered in God and God's action, through Jesus Christ, and not in human-centered initiatives. Therefore, his main impact in the spiritual realm was in the spheres of Catholic and Lutheran-Protestant life. That directly involves a billion Catholics and, in more complex and sprawling ways beyond Lutheranism, hundreds of millions of Protestant lives. If this effect is somewhat less decisive now in cultures called "secular" and "pluralist," it continues in them and is being enriched in places far from Euro-America. These include southern Africa, South and Central America, and Asia.

Why this wide effect and appeal? Luther would have answered: because the heart of his theology and practice reached the human heart at its deepest fonts. In a sense, what he discovered by searching his soul was that the inner world, the relation to God, colored everything among thoughtful people, beginning with his observation of himself. How they acted in the world, what they practiced in the realm of the spirit, what they hoped for, was cramped and devastated if one was not in a positive relation to a gracious God, or it led to a life of freedom and delight. His key to experiencing the difference came with attitudes to repentance and the practice of repenting. His focus on this, so well summarized in the first of the Ninety-Five Theses, which appeared "on or about" October 31, which he either posted on a door at the university or mailed to his archbishop about then.

Catholics and other Christians in the twenty-first century know that they do not live in the little Wittenberg and big Rome of 1517, though some may act as if they do. However much the actions of Luther and his counterparts "changed the world," the world, of course, keeps changing apart from them. For that reason, many Catholics, Lutherans, and other Protestants are using the "quincentenary" year to repent—that's the key word in the first of the Ninety-Five Theses—in all of their life, but also with specific focus on Christian unity and sins against it. As far as "all of life" is concerned, they may have difficulty seeing themselves in the context of Luther's problems about guilt and divine wrath and punishment, so they may not be seeking his solution, his address to them.

To some people of God there has to be a question: Why take on the problems that moved Luther and others to deal as they did with repentance? Life is difficult enough without the attempt to retrofit themselves into the thought world of a sixteenth-century monk who had troubles with God. Luther left plenty of testimony that he was severely troubled. The devil was real to him, and never more so than in the darkness of night, when the tired scholar and teacher sought solace and found none. His God might save him, but this God has to be experienced as a judge over each sinner—and all are sinners—who keeps score as if in an account book, and will judge, even to the point of eternal punishment. Graphic art from Luther's time was often grotesquely devoted to depicting this. A familiar image was that of the *Totentanz*, the skeleton-filled "dance of death."

No wonder Luther was a scrupulous, almost fanatic confessor. His generous main confessor in the Augustinian monastery, Johannes Staupitz, had to hear Luther tear himself up spiritually in efforts to clear his record before God. It may be hard for moderns to empathize with someone in a monastery who had available all the sacred hours and devices one needed to confess, but poor Staupitz heard hour after hour of confession to the point that he once complained to Luther that he did not have to confess every fart. Whether or not Luther was mentally unbalanced or whether he was a genius at self-examination, a sort of Mozart-level genius at confession, as it were, he certainly was not modeling the life of belief in a gracious God.

A gracious God! Finding one was his desperate search. Five-hundred years later, one has to ask (and I confess, I have to ask), does the sinner need all that scrupulosity and self-obsession? Where is God in all this? Contemporary theologians who examine their hearts and look around them wrestle with the question: What if I am not as tortured as Luther and Luther-types were by guilt and with images and experiences of God as a threatening terror?

So the question is: *Must* one experience young Luther's agonies over a distant, hidden, or merely threatening God in order to repent effectively? The stress here is on the "young" Luther, because there are other Luthers, other expressions of this Luther. He was not only that tortured soul, though he never obscured his awareness of sin. We have read his formula: the human is both "justified" and a "sinner," simultaneously. The Scriptures on which Luther relied portray many other pictures of humans-before-God than this one. And theologians sometimes question the Christians who are mired in guilt. Thus Dietrich Bonhoeffer, a prophet executed by Nazis, wanted Christians to deal with humans not only in their weakness but also in their strength. Otherwise they would just be dealing with existentialist philosophers, psychotherapists, and "secularized Methodists." And theologian Paul Tillich noted that guilt and the search for a *gracious* God now was transformed into a search for God and for meaning in life.

In addition to questioning the image of the tortured sinner, one has to ask in the context of this Catholic-Lutheran dialogue: How much spiritual energy should Christians devote to repentance over disunity among Christians in various communities? It is encouraging to see how planners for the commemorations five hundred years after 1517 called for repentance because of the disunity, conflicts, and separations, in one particular case, between Lutherans and Catholics. My earlier reference to philosopher Max Scheler throws some light on this. Picture a new convert from agnosticism or apathy to Christianity, one who is drawn to the Catholic or Lutheran church (or other Protestant counterparts). Suppose he or she is confronted at once by the call to repent over centuries of backbiting, undercutting, and misusing of the other across the boundaries of the communions.

If we listen to such a convert, we are sure to hear expressions of regret for actions from 1517 to the present. Quite often we may hear questions of what to do because of disunity. But, Scheler-style, we know that the past is past. It does not exist. It cannot be changed. What *can* be changed is one's attitude. What kinds of sinners in need of repentance were our separated and often bitterly critical ancestors? No; a second question gets us closer: What kind of person am I that I can now still contribute to the flaws in the life of the divided churches? But, better, the believer is tutored to ask: What kind of person am I that I am capable of contributing to division within the *one*, holy, Catholic, and apostolic church? That question deserves and allows for a positive, not joyless, act of repentance.

When believers ask such and thus repent and want to change, in the light of the day in 1517 that "changed the world," they can be and will be positioned to experience change and then to change. They will weep in each other's misfortunes and weaknesses, but they will also rejoice in the fruits of common dialogue, common prayer, and joint action. It all depends on the Holy Spirit and "a change of heart."

APPENDIX

# THE
# Ninety-five
# Theses

I N THE DESIRE AND WITH THE PURPOSE of making the truth clear, a setting forth of theses will be held on the propositions shown below at Wittenberg, under the presidency of the Reverend Father Martin Luther, Monk of the Order of St. Augustine, Master of Arts and of Sacred Theology, and ordinary Reader of the same in that place. In the name of our Lord Jesus Christ. Amen.

1. When our Lord and Master Jesus Christ said "Repent," he intended the entire life of believers to be repentance.*

2. This word cannot be understood as sacramental penance, that is, as the confession and satisfaction that are performed under the ministry of priests.

3. It does not, however, refer solely to inward penitence; indeed, such inward penitence is nothing, unless it outwardly produces various mortifications of the flesh.

*EDITOR'S NOTE: Luther's text gave Christ's words as *agite poenitentiam*, from the Latin Vulgate. This term is rendered here as *Repent*. But there is another aspect of the word. The effect of the ninety-five theses depends on the double meaning of *poenitentia*: repentance—an inner turning from sin; and penance—outward actions that show proof of one's repentance.

4. Therefore the penalty continues as long as the hatred of self—that is, true inward penitence—continues; namely, till our entrance into the kingdom of heaven.

5. The Pope has neither the will nor the power to remit any penalties, except those that he has imposed by his own authority, or by that of the canons.

6. The Pope has no power to remit any guilt, except by declaring and warranting it to have been remitted by God; or at most by remitting cases reserved for himself. In those cases, if his power were despised, guilt would certainly remain.

7. God never remits anyone's guilt without at the same time subjecting that person, humbled in all things, to the authority of God's representative the priest.

8. The penitential canons are imposed only on the living, and no burden ought to be imposed on the dying, according to them.

9. Therefore the Holy Spirit acting in the Pope does well for us, in that, in his decrees, he always makes exception of the article of death and of necessity.

10. Those priests act wrongly and without learning, who, in the case of the dying, reserve the canonical penances for purgatory.

11. The sowing of weeds about changing the canonical penalty into the penalty of purgatory seems surely to have been done while the bishops were asleep.

12. Formerly the canonical penalties were imposed not after, but before absolution, as tests of true contrition.

13. The dying pay all penalties by death, and are already dead to the canon laws, and are by right relieved from them.

14. The imperfect soundness or love of a dying person necessarily brings with it great fear, and the less it is, the greater the fear it brings.

15. This fear and horror is sufficient by itself, to say nothing of other things, to constitute the pains of purgatory, since it is very near to the horror of despair.

16. Hell, purgatory, and heaven appear to differ just as despair, almost despair, and peace of mind differ.

17. With souls in purgatory it seems that it must be that, as horror diminishes, so love increases.

18. Nor does it seem to be proved by any reasoning or any Scriptures, that they are outside of the state of merit or of the increase of love.

19. Nor does it appear to be proved that they are sure and confident of their own blessedness, at least not all of them, though we may be very sure of it.

20. Therefore the Pope, when he speaks of the full remission of all penalties, does not mean every single type of penalty, but only of those imposed by himself.

21. Therefore those preachers of indulgences are in error who say that, by the indulgences of the Pope, a person is made exempt and saved from all punishment.

22. For in fact the Pope remits to souls in purgatory no penalty that, according to the canons, they would have had to pay in this life.

23. If any entire remission of all penalties can be granted to anyone, it is certain that it is granted only to the most perfect, that is, to very few.

24. Therefore a great number of people must be deceived by this indiscriminate and high-sounding promise of release from penalties.

25. The power that the Pope has over purgatory in general is the same as that of every bishop in his own diocese, and every curate in his own parish, in particular.

26. The Pope acts most rightly in granting remission to souls, not by the power of the keys (which does not apply in the case of purgatory) but by way of intercession for them.

27. They preach only vain human doctrines who say that the soul flies out of purgatory as soon as money thrown into the chest clinks.

28. It is certain that when money clinks in the chest, avarice and greed may increase, but the intercession of the Church depends on the will of God alone.

29. Who knows whether all the souls in purgatory desire to be redeemed from it, according to the story told of Saints Severinus and Paschal.

30. None are sure of the reality of their own contrition, much less of the attainment of full remission of sins.

31. As rare as a true penitent is, so rare is one who truly gains indulgences—that is to say, exceedingly rare.

32. Those who believe that through letters of indulgence they are made sure of their own salvation, will be eternally damned along with their teachers.

33. We must especially be on guard against those who say that these indulgences from the Pope are

the inestimable gift of God by which humans are reconciled to God.

34. For the grace conveyed by these indulgences has respect only to the penalties of sacramental satisfaction, which are of human appointment.

35. People do not preach any kind of Christian doctrine who teach that sorrow for sin and repentance are not necessary for those who buy souls out of purgatory or buy letters of indulgence.

36. Every Christian who feels sincere repentance and sorrow for sin has perfect remission of pain and guilt even without letters of indulgence.

37. Any true Christian, whether living or dead, participates in all the blessings of Christ and the Church, and this is granted by God, even without letters of indulgence.

38. Nonetheless, the remission of sin imparted by the Pope is in no way to be despised, since it is, as I have said, a declaration of the Divine remission.

39. It is a most difficult thing, even for the most learned theologians, to hold up in the eyes of the people the ample effect of indulgences and at the same time the necessity of true sorrow for sin and repentance.

40. Those who are truly sorry for sin and repent for it seek and love to pay penalties for sin; while the abundance of indulgences softens penalties and causes people to hate them, or at least it gives occasion for them to do so.

41. Papal indulgences ought to be proclaimed with caution, so that people will not falsely suppose that they are placed before other good works of love.

42. Christians should be taught that it is not the mind of the Pope that buying indulgences is to be in any way compared to works of mercy.

43. Christians should be taught that people who give to a poor person, or lend to a needy person, do better than if they bought indulgences.

44. For, by the exercise of love, love increases and people become better; by contrast, by means of indulgences they do not become better, but only freer from punishment.

45. Christians should be taught that those who see another in need and pass on by, and then give money for indulgences, are not purchasing for themselves the Pope's indulgences, but rather God's anger.

46. Christians should be taught that unless they have more than enough wealth, they are duty bound to keep what is necessary for the use of their own households, and by no means to lavish it on indulgences.

47. Christians should be taught that, while they are free to buy indulgences, they are not commanded to do so.

48. Christians should be taught that the Pope, in selling indulgences, has both more need and more desire for devout prayer to be made for him, than for the free flow of money.

49. Christians should be taught that the Pope's indulgences are useful if they do not put their trust in them, but most hurtful if through them they lose the fear of God.

50. Christians should be taught that if the Pope were acquainted with the unjust demands for contributions levied by the preachers of indulgences, he would much rather that the Basilica of St. Peter should be burned to ashes, than that it should be built up with the skin, flesh, and bones of his sheep.

51. Christians should be taught that, as it would be the duty, so it would be the wish of the Pope, even to sell, if necessary, the Basilica of St. Peter, and to give of his own money to very many of those from whom the hawkers of indulgences extort money.

52. It is vain to hope for salvation through letters of indulgence, even if a person delegated to grant them—yes, even the Pope himself—were to pledge his own soul for them.

53. They are enemies of Christ and of the Pope, who, in order to preach sermons about indulgences, condemn the word of God to utter silence in other churches.

54. Wrong is done to the word of God when, in the same sermon, an equal or longer time is spent on indulgences than on the word of God.

55. The mind of the Pope must be that if indulgences, which are of small importance, are celebrated with single bells, single processions, and single ceremonies, then the Gospel, which is of very great importance, should be preached with a hundred bells, a hundred processions, and a hundred ceremonies.

56. The treasures of the Church, out of which the Pope grants indulgences, are neither sufficiently named nor sufficiently known among the people of Christ.

57. It is clear that they are at least not temporal treasures, for these are not so readily lavished, but only accumulated, by many of the sellers of indulgences.

58. Nor are they the merits of Christ and of the saints, for these, independently of the Pope, are always working grace in the inner self, and the cross, death, and hell in the outer self.

59. St. Lawrence said that the poor are the treasures of the Church, but he spoke according to the use of the word in his time.

60. We are not speaking rashly when we say that the keys of the Church, bestowed through the merits of Christ, are that treasure.

61. For it is clear that the Pope's power is sufficient in itself for the remission of penalties in cases reserved for the Pope.

62. The true treasure of the Church is the Holy Gospel of the glory and grace of God.

63. This treasure, however, is odious to human nature, because it makes the first to be last.

64. But the treasure of indulgences is most acceptable to human nature, because it makes the last to be first.

65. Therefore the treasures of the Gospel are nets that in past times were used to fish for people of wealth.

66. The treasures of indulgences are nets that are now used to fish for the wealth of people.

67. The indulgences that the preachers loudly proclaim to be the greatest graces are to be understood as such only insofar as they promote gain.

68. Yet they are in reality in no way to be compared to the grace of God and the devotion of the cross.

69. Bishops and curates are duty bound to receive the sellers of papal indulgences with all reverence.

70. But they are still more duty bound to see to it with their own eyes, and take heed with their own ears, that these men do not preach their own dreams in place of what the Pope has commanded.

71. Those who speak against the truth concerning papal indulgences must be declared anathema and accursed.

72. But on the other hand, those who guard against the extravagant claims and license of speech of the preachers of indulgences, are to be blessed.

73. Just as the Pope justly thunders against those who use any kind of contrivance to threaten the traffic in indulgences,

74. Much more is it his intention to thunder against those who, using indulgences as a pretext, contrive to harm holy love and truth.

75. To think that Papal indulgences have such power that they could absolve a person even if—by an impossibility—that person had violated the Mother of God, is madness.

76. We affirm on the contrary that Papal indulgences cannot take away even the least of venial sins, as regards their guilt.

77. To say that even if St. Peter were now Pope he could grant no greater graces, is blasphemy against St. Peter and the Pope.

78. We affirm on the contrary that both he and any other Pope has greater graces to grant, namely, the Gospel, powers, gifts of healing, and the like, as it is written (1 Corinthians 12:9).

79. To say that the cross emblazoned with the papal coat of arms is equal in worth to the cross of Christ is blasphemy.

80. Those bishops, curates, and theologians who allow such arguments to be uttered among the people, will have to render an account for this.

81. This unbridled preaching of indulgences makes it no easy thing, even for learned persons, to protect the reverence due to the Pope against the false and malicious statements, or, in any event, the shrewd questionings of the laity.

82. As, for instance: Why does not the Pope empty purgatory for the sake of most holy love and of the supreme necessity of souls—this being the most just of all reasons—if he redeems an infinite number of souls for the sake of that most miserable thing, money, to be spent on building a basilica? The former would be most just; the latter is most trivial.

83. Again: Why do funeral masses and anniversary masses for the deceased continue, and why does not the Pope return, or permit the withdrawal of the funds bequeathed for this purpose, since it is wrong to pray for those who are already redeemed?

84. Again: What is this new kindness of God and the Pope, in that, for money's sake, they permit an irreligious person and an enemy of God to redeem a devout soul that loves God, and yet do not redeem that same devout and beloved soul, out of free love, on account of its own need?

85. Again: Why is it that the canons of penance, long since abolished and dead in actual fact and not

only by disuse, are nonetheless still redeemed with money, through the granting of indulgences, as if they were still alive and in use?

86. Again: Why does not the Pope, whose riches today are ampler than those of the wealthiest of the wealthy, build this one Basilica of St. Peter with his own money, rather than with that of poor believers?

87. Again: What does the Pope remit or impart to those who, through perfect sorrow for sin and repentance, have a right to full remission and blessing?

88. Again: What greater good would the Church receive if the Pope, instead of once, as he does now, were to bestow these remissions and blessings a hundred times a day on any one of the faithful?

89. Since it is the salvation of souls, rather than money, that the Pope seeks by his indulgences, why does he suspend the letters and indulgences granted long ago, since they are equally effective?

90. To repress these misgivings and arguments of the laity by force alone, and not to solve them by giving reasons, is to expose the Church and the Pope to the ridicule of their enemies and to make Christians unhappy.

91. If, therefore, forgiveness of sin were preached according to the spirit and mind of the Pope, all these questions would be resolved with ease; indeed, they would not exist.

92. Away, then, with all those prophets who say to the people of Christ: "Peace, peace," and there is no peace (Jeremiah 6:14).

93. Blessed be all those prophets who say to the people of Christ: "The cross, the cross," and there is no cross.

94. Christians should be exhorted to strive to follow Christ, their Head, through penalties, deaths, and hells.

95. And by this they should trust to enter heaven through many severe tribulations, rather than through the security of peace.

3   *"any real book. . . ."*: Eugen Rosenstock-Huessy, *Out of Revolution: Autobiography of Western Man* (Norwich, CT: Argo, 1969), 13.

9   For the Max Scheler reference, see Peter H. Spader, "A Change of Heart: Scheler's *Ordo Amoris*, Repentance and Rebirth," *Listening: Journal of Religion and Culture*, 21, no. 3 (fall 1986): 188–96.

14   *"decisive historical changes. . . ."*: José Ortega y Gasset quotation. Quoted in Karl J. Weintraub, *Visions of Culture* (Chicago: University of Chicago Press, 1966), 269.

26   *"The Lutheran Church of China. . . ."*: See E. Theodore Bachmann and Mercia Brenne Bachmann, *The Lutheran Churches in the World* (Minneapolis: Augsburg, 1989), 162.

35   *"'Catholic' is commonly said to mean. . . ."*: Walter Ong, SJ, "Yeast: A Parable for Catholic Higher Education," *America*, April 7, 1990.

37 *"By soul I mean nothing mystical or religious, . . ."*: Leon
Kass, *Toward a More Natural Science: Biology and Human
Affairs* (New York: Free Press, 1988), chap. 10.

96 *Therefore the penalty continues*: This refers to *poena*
(pain, punishment, penalty), again suggesting the
connection between *poena* and *poenitentia*.

## Who We Are

Paraclete Press is a publisher of books, recordings, and DVDs on Christian spirituality. Our publishing represents a full expression of Christian belief and practice—from Catholic to Evangelical, from Protestant to Orthodox.

We are the publishing arm of the Community of Jesus, an ecumenical monastic community in the Benedictine tradition. As such, we are uniquely positioned in the marketplace without connection to a large corporation and with informal relationships to many branches and denominations of faith.

## What We Are Doing

### PARACLETE PRESS BOOKS

Paraclete publishes books that show the richness and depth of what it means to be Christian. Although Benedictine spirituality is at the heart of who we are and all that we do, we publish books that reflect the Christian experience across many cultures, time periods, and houses of worship. We publish books that nourish the vibrant life of the church and its people.

We have several different series, including the bestselling Paraclete Essentials and Paraclete Giants series of classic texts in contemporary English; Voices from the Monastery—men and women monastics writing about living a spiritual life today; our award-winning Paraclete Poetry series as well as the Mount Tabor Books on the arts; bestselling gift books for children on the occasions of baptism and first communion; and the Active Prayer Series that brings creativity and liveliness to any life of prayer.

*Prayers of the Reformers*
THOMAS McPHERSON

ISBN 978-1-61261-927-9 | $12.99 PAPERBACK

In this 500th anniversary year of the Reformation, this volume collects the writing of well-known reformers Martin Luther, John Calvin, John Knox, Thomas Cranmer, Lancelot Andrewes, as well as lesser-known leaders of their time. Rather than look at the theological arguments and apologetics of these religious thinkers, we instead look to their hopes and concerns by reading their prayers.

This year, many are asking, "How is the Reformation relevant for today?" These prayers, arranged by author and subject, will open a window into the personal faith and spirituality of those on the front lines of that great upheaval in the church and culture. Their wisdom speaks across the centuries to our world today, torn by competing religious and political factions and challenges to the institutions of faith.